BIBLE TRAVELS

Fun Pad

developed by Scoti Domeij and Greg Holder
illustrated by Raleigh Swanson

Travels of Paul

STANDARD PUBLISHING
Cincinnati, Ohio

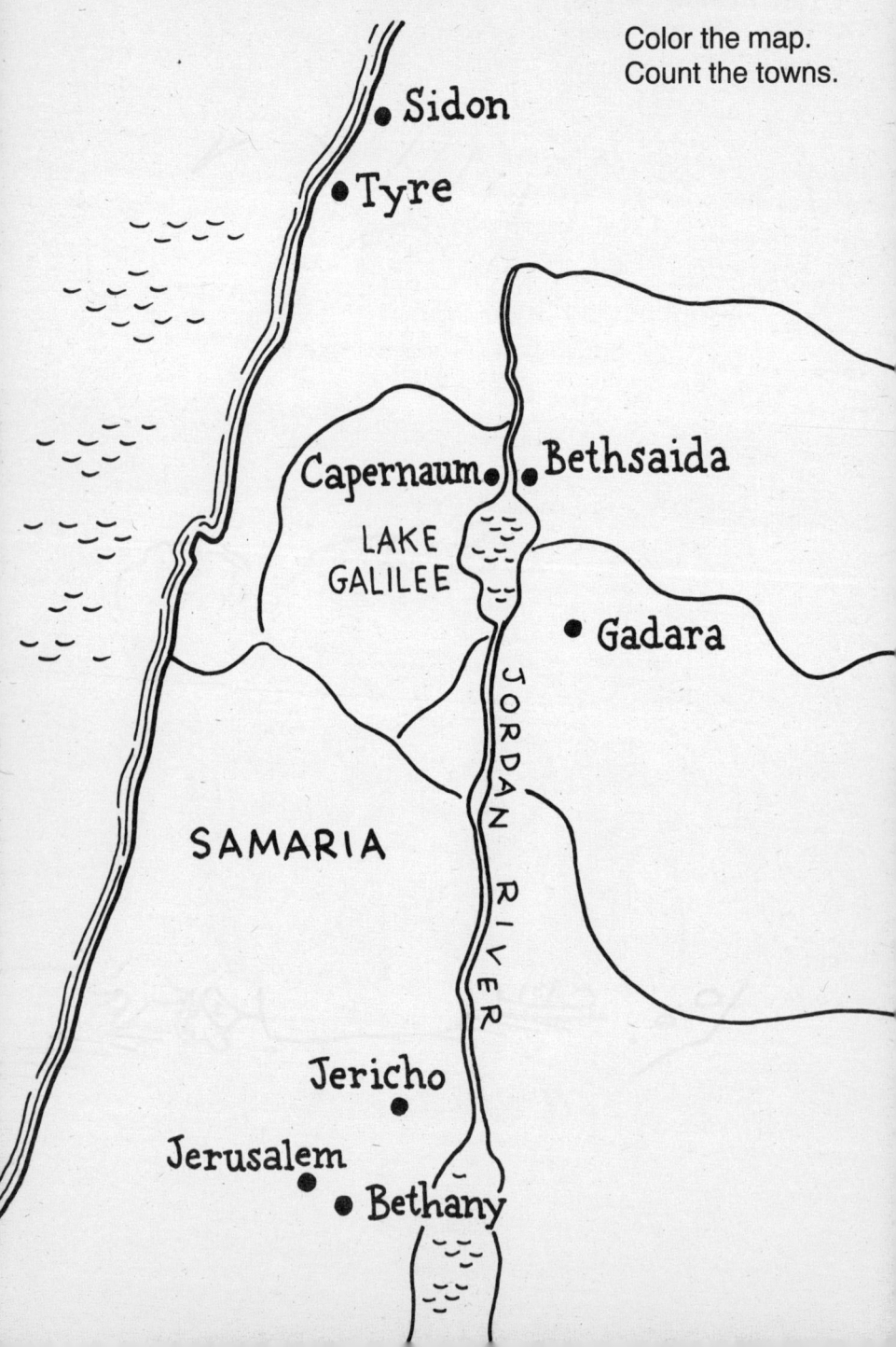

Number Code

Jesus rode into the city of Jerusalem on a donkey. Use the number code to find out what the people shouted as he rode by.

1=D 2=P 3=O 4=R 5=G 6=A 7=E 8=I 9=S

__ __ __ __ __ __ __ __ __ !
2 4 6 8 9 7   5 3 1

Answer: Praise God!

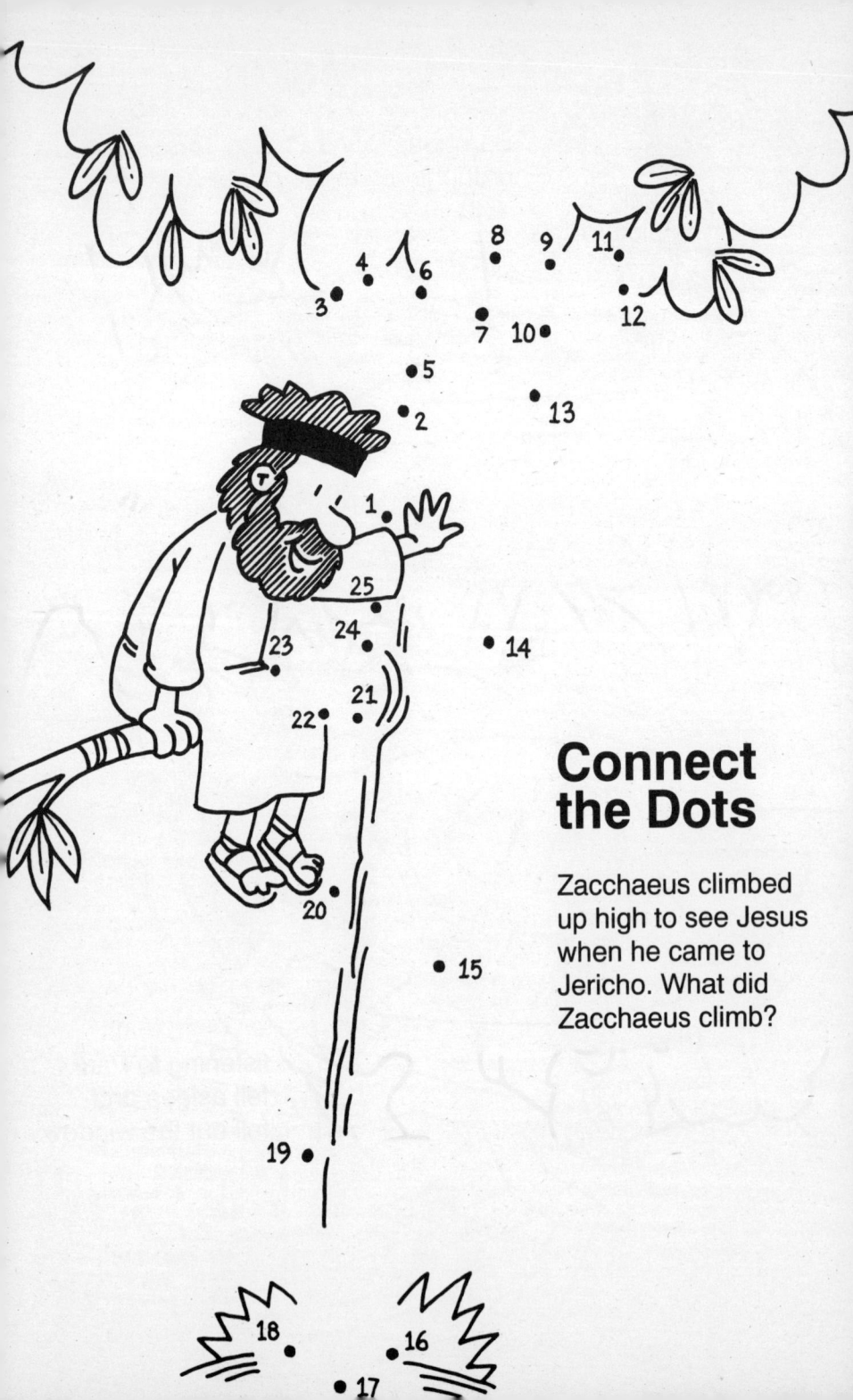

Connect the Dots

Zacchaeus climbed up high to see Jesus when he came to Jericho. What did Zacchaeus climb?

Number Code

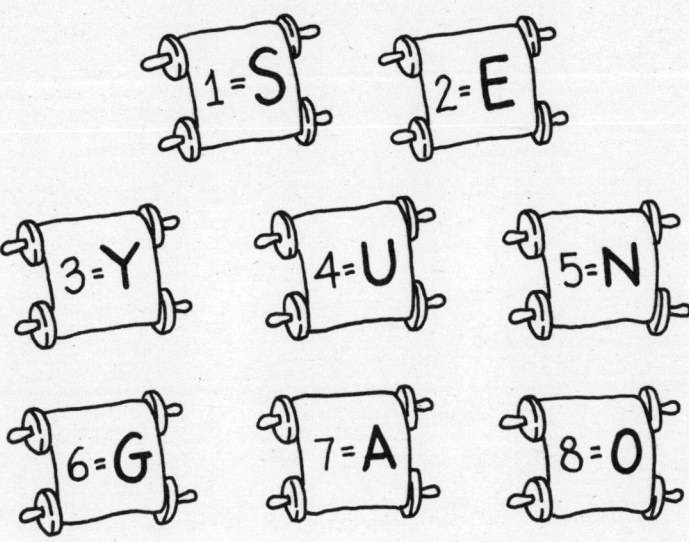

In the city of Antioch, Paul preached in the

_____.

Use the number code to discover the name of this place.

Answer: synagogue

Hidden Word

On the road to Samaria, Jesus healed ten men. Only one man gave praise to God. What did the man say to Jesus? Color the spaces with the dots.

Answer: Thank you

Word Search

In Lystra, people thought Paul and Barnabas were the Greek gods Zeus and Hermes.

A	L	Y	S	T	R	A
V	M	U	W	A	O	B
M	R	F	D	S	Y	A
P	Q	O	W	I	E	R
F	L	S	K	A	J	N
S	P	A	U	L	I	A
U	B	H	B	J	M	B
E	Z	W	X	E	C	A
Z	H	E	R	M	E	S

Find these names in the puzzle.
Look up, across, and down.

LYSTRA   ZEUS
PAUL   HERMES
BARNABAS

Word Scramble

In Bethany, Jesus brought Lazarus back to life.
Unscramble the words to see what Jesus said.

_ _ _ _ _ _ _ , _ _ _ _   _ _ _ !

Answer: Lazarus, come out!

Find the Baskets

After Jesus fed the crowd near Bethsaida, there were twelve baskets of leftovers. Find the baskets in the picture.

Fish Match-Up

Near Bethsaida, Jesus fed many people with just one boy's small lunch. Find the two mirror fish. Circle the bread that is different.

Use the Code

In Philippi, Paul and Silas went to jail for telling people about Jesus. What time was it when they were praying and singing and God sent an earthquake to rescue them?

Answer: midnight

Word Search

Near Tyre and Sidon, Jesus healed a woman's sick daughter. Find these words in the puzzle. Look up, across, and down.

JESUS   TYRE   SIDON   DAUGHTER   HEAL

D	H	E	A	L	J	R
F	N	C	E	G	Y	D
Q	P	D	R	V	M	A
J	I	C	Y	K	A	U
E	C	N	T	J	D	G
S	M	E	O	F	E	H
U	T	U	R	I	F	T
S	S	I	D	O	N	E
L	K	J	H	G	F	R

Connect the Dots

The people who heard Paul preach in Berea checked the Scriptures to see if Paul was telling them the truth. What were the Scriptures written on?

Picture Code

In the land of Gadara, evil spirits begged Jesus to send them into a herd of _____ . Write the first letter of each picture to find out what the animals were.

___ ___ ___ ___
 1   2   3   4

Answer: pigs

Rebus Crossword

In 🏘 Capernaum, 👤 Jesus healed the 👳 servant of a Roman 🪖 soldier. Write the name of each picture in the correct spaces.

Finish the Picture

Paul worked as a tentmaker in Corinth. Finish the tent.

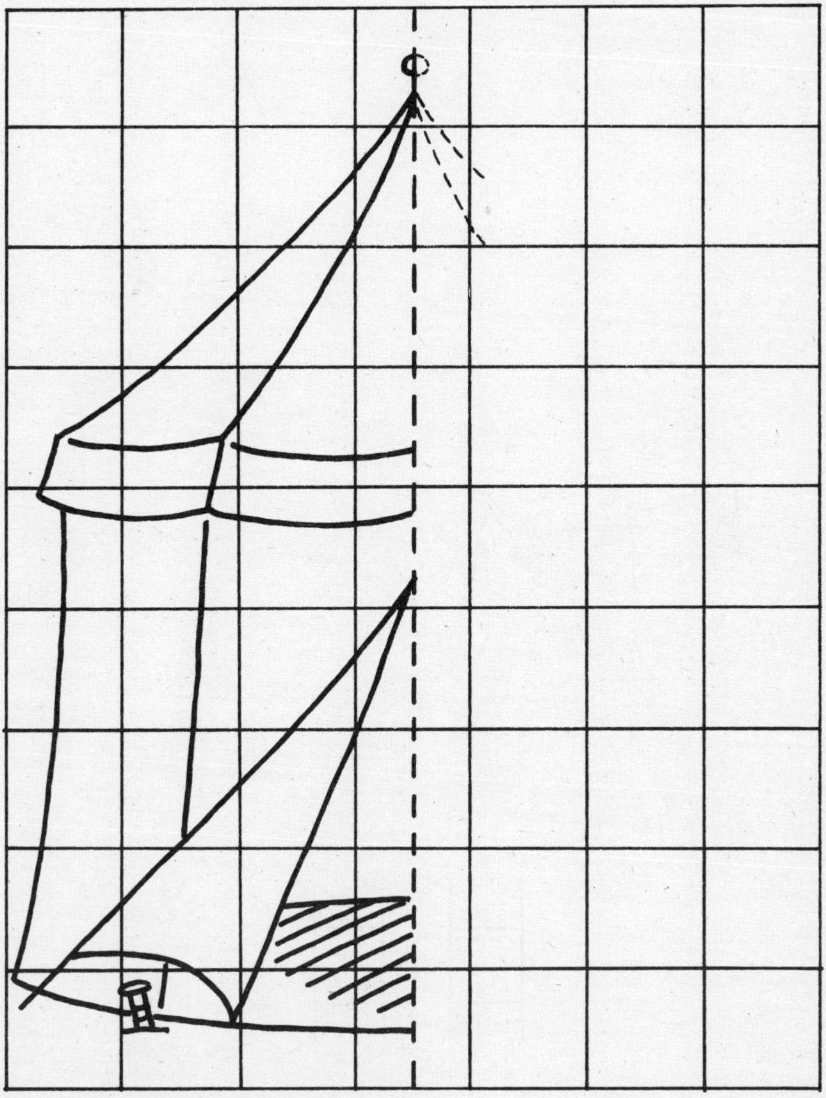

Jesus Match-Up

Jesus went to the Jordan River to be baptized by John. Circle the pictures of Jesus and John that are the same.

Word Search

On the way to Rome, Paul was shipwrecked on an island called Malta. Find these words in the puzzle. Look up, across, and down.

ROME   PAUL   MALTA   ISLAND

M	A	L	T	A	J	S
Q	P	W	O	E	D	R
R	L	D	K	S	N	A
O	Z	E	X	C	A	T
M	M	O	N	I	L	U
E	U	H	Y	G	S	F
F	P	A	U	L	I	A
V	G	C	D	N	J	X
Z	G	X	H	C	I	W

Word Wheel

For two years in Rome, Paul lived in his own rented _____ . Write the first letter of each picture to finish the sentence.

__ __ __ __ __
1 2 3 4 5

Answer: house

Where's Paul?

Many people in the places Paul visited became believers in Jesus. Can you find Paul in this crowd?

BIBLE TRAVELS

Fun Pad

developed by Scoti Domeij and Greg Holder
illustrated by Raleigh Swanson

Journeys of Jesus

STANDARD PUBLISHING
Cincinnati, Ohio